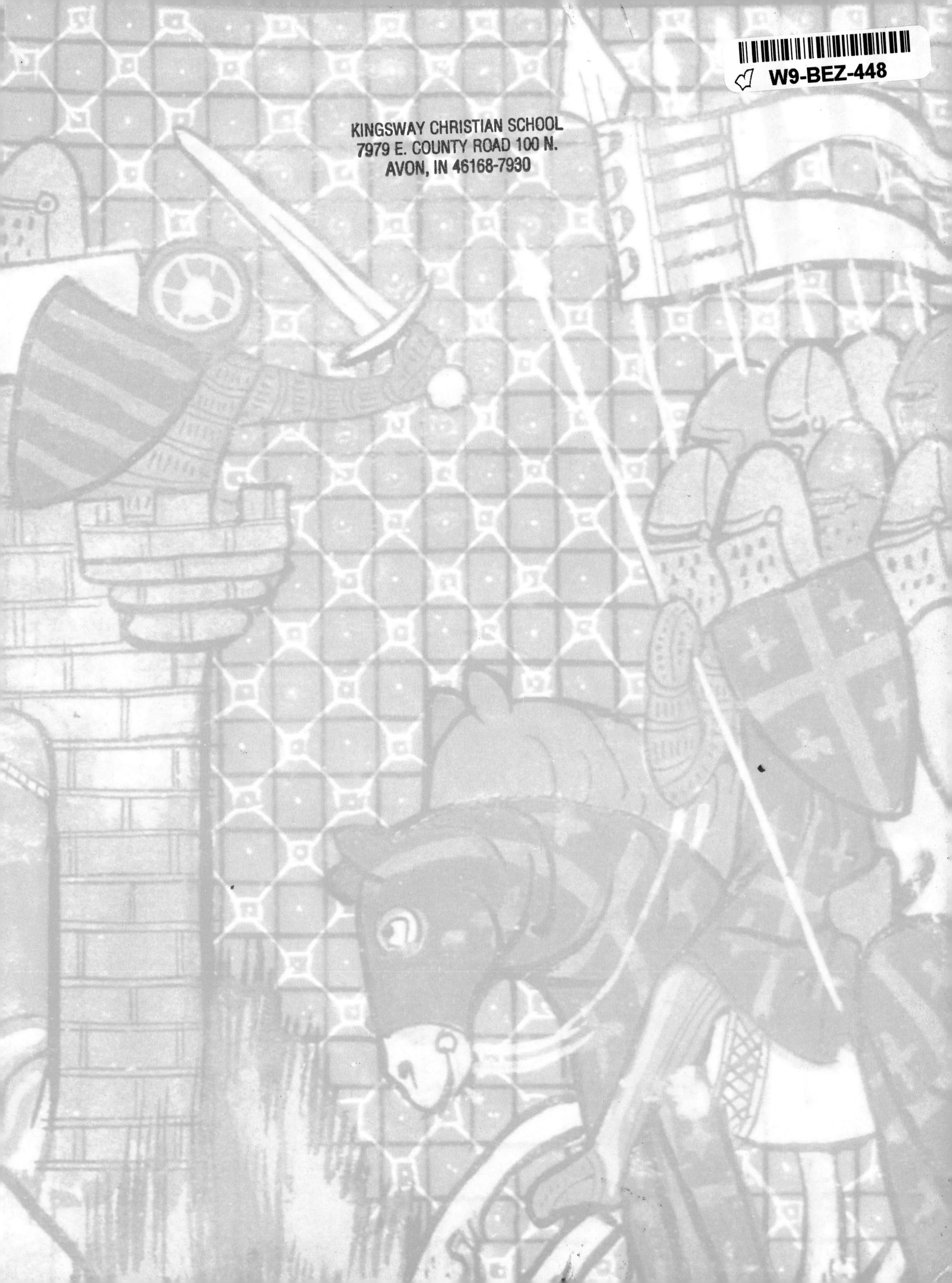

CASTLES

Philip Steele

NEW YORK

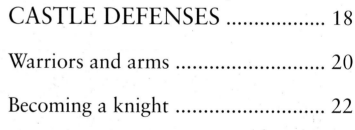

KINGFISHER
Larousse Kingfisher Chambers Inc.
95 Madison Avenue
New York, New York 10016

First American edition 1995
10 9 8 7 6 5

Library of Congress
Cataloging-in-Publication Data

Steele, Philip,
  Castles / Philip Steele—1st American ed.
  p. cm.
  Includes index.
  1. Castles—Juvenile literature. I. Title
3T3550.S74 1995
  940.1–dc20 94–29366 CIP AC

ISBN 1-85697-547-9

Author: Philip Steele
Consultant: Brian Davison
Series editor: Sue Nicholson
Editor: Clive Wilson
Design: Ben White Associates
Cover design: John Jamieson
Art editor: Christina Fraser
Picture research: Elaine Willis
Typeset by Karen Sage
Printed in Italy

CONTENTS

Title page: A great banquet in the early 1400s, from the Duke of Berry's *Très Riches Heures*.

THE AGE OF CASTLES

The great age of castles began almost 1,000 years ago and lasted for nearly 500 years. During this time, over 15,000 castles stretched across the lands of Europe and the Near East. They towered over the valleys of the Rhine in Germany and the Seine in France. They guarded lonely mountain passes in Scotland and Wales. They were battered and besieged in the scorching heat of Spain, Sicily, and Syria.

Crusader castle

The castle of Krak des Chevaliers was originally an Arab fortress. It was taken over and rebuilt by Christian knights during the wars of the Crusades. These took place in the 1100s and 1200s when Christians fought against Muslims called Saracens.

▼ Krak was a military base which could hold over 2,000 men. Its powerful defenses survived 12 sieges before it was finally captured in 1271.

▲ In times of peace, a castle's lord and lady held great feasts and wore their finest clothes.

Castles were built in an age of war. These powerful strongholds were used to control and defend large areas of the surrounding countryside. They were a base from which a lord and his soldiers could launch attacks on their enemies. With their high towers and thick walls, castles also provided protection against the fiercest of enemy assaults. But a castle was much more than a fortress. Inside its walls there might be a magnificent hall, comfortable chambers, and a beautiful chapel. A castle was the home of its lord, his family, and his followers— and they could live there in style.

People and power

In the Middle Ages, land was the key to power and wealth— and land was controlled from castles. The most powerful person in the kingdom was the king. He allowed his nobles to hold land if they promised to support him against his enemies. In turn, the nobles gave parts of their land to other knights who promised to fight for them. This arrangement of giving land in return for loyalty or service is called the feudal system, or feudalism.

king

queen

Turbulent times

The Middle Ages started when the Roman Empire, which had united most of Europe, broke up in the 470s. Fierce fighting followed, and Europe became a land of small, warring kingdoms. Over the years, some of these kingdoms became very powerful and took over the weaker ones. By the 1450s, when the Middle Ages ended, some of the countries we know today were beginning to take shape.

By order of the king!

The king's word was law. If he wanted to, he could have you thrown into jail or your head chopped off!

Orders sent by the king were tied with cord and marked with a great wax seal showing the royal stamp. Refusal to obey the king's orders was an act of rebellion and could be punished by death.

◄ The seal of King John of England, who reigned from 1199 to 1216.

bishop   lord   lady   knight   merchant   nun

peasant

Working life

Workers included crafts-men, such as blacksmiths, merchants, who bought and sold goods, and peasants, who worked the land.

Three classes

In the Middle Ages, society was strictly divided into three groups. People either fought, prayed, or worked for their living.

Top to bottom

Every person knew their place. The king gave orders to the lords, the lords gave orders to the knights, and everyone gave orders to the poor peasants!

Fighting men

The lords and the knights defended the king from his enemies. From the 1200s, however, the king often accepted money from them rather than make them fight.

Religious life

In Europe, most people were Christians. Many churches and cathedrals were built and most castles had their own chapel.

On the move

Kings and wealthy lords had more than one castle—King John had over one hundred! They traveled from one to another with their soldiers, servants, and wagons.

7

Building a castle

 It is the year 1290, and a great stone castle is being built. There are no power tools or bulldozers as there are on a modern building site. Most of the work is done by muscle power. Carpenters saw wood and assemble the scaffolding. Blacksmiths make and fix tools. Masons shape stone, and laborers curse and sweat as they haul heavy loads, mix up mortar for the walls, and dig trenches.

Mason's marks

Every mason had his own special mark. He often carved this design into the stone he was working on, a bit like a painter signing a painting. The marks were also used to work out how much each mason should be paid.

Raising the walls

Scaffolding was made of wood (1). It was slotted into openings in the stonework called putlog holes (2). For extra strength, a castle's main walls were packed with stone rubble and flints mixed with mortar (3). Walls could be between 6 and 16 feet thick.

Masons

A master mason was hired to design the castle and take charge of its building (4). Directly under him were freemasons, who cut and carved the stone (5), and roughmasons, who built the walls (6).

Lifting loads

Ropes and pulleys were used to lift buckets of materials and beams (7). Heavy stones were raised by a treadwheel crane, which was turned by a man walking inside a giant wheel (8).

8

Working army

An army of workers was needed to build a castle. In 1295, 30 blacksmiths, 400 masons, and 2,000 laborers, including stone-breakers and well-diggers, were hired to build Beaumaris Castle in North Wales.

laborers

carpenter

blacksmiths

mason

About 1,000 years ago, castles were built from wood. This was soon replaced by stone, which was stronger and could not be burned down by an enemy. Planning these stone castles was a difficult job. Building supplies and materials had to be brought in by river, sea, or land. Masons had to be hired and laborers organized. A castle could take 10 or sometimes even 20 years to complete, and in today's money it would cost several million dollars.

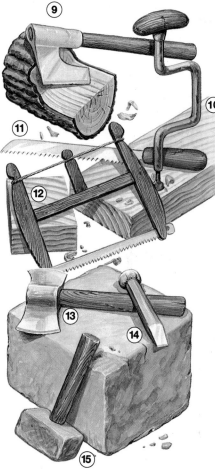

Tools of the trade

A carpenter used an ax (9), an awl (10), a saw (11), and a handsaw (12). A mason used a mason's ax (13), a chisel (14), and a mallet (15).

9

Clues to the past

Today, most castles lie empty or in ruins. Their defenses are shattered, their walls bare, and their great halls silent, except perhaps for the whistling wind. However, with a little detective work it's easy to find clues and work out what a castle looked like in the Middle Ages.

1 The keep
It's usually easy to find the keep—the largest building standing in the heart of the castle. Its outer walls would have once been whitened with lime to dazzle the eye.

2 Stone walls
In some castles you may see a trace of faded colored plaster on the inside walls. This plaster was once painted with bold, colorful patterns or hung with richly woven tapestries.

3 The gatehouse
Grooves in the wall at the entrance show where the portcullis was raised and lowered. The portcullis slid down the grooves to make a gate. Behind were two heavy wooden doors.

So why did so many castles become ruins? By the end of the 1400s wars were being fought in open country, not around castles, and kings and nobles no longer needed to live in fortified homes. Instead, they chose to live in more comfortable houses, and castles were left empty and deserted.

4 Fireplaces

High up in the walls are the remains of fireplaces. Look for rows of small square holes beneath them. These once held joists—the timbers that supported the floors.

5 The chapel

Where was the castle chapel? Look for rows of arched windows, finely carved stonework, and a stone basin in one of the walls. The basin would have held water to rinse the cup used during religious services.

6 Wall defenses

Can you see holes in the stonework of the outer walls? In times of war these supported the beams of wooden platforms called hourds.

7 Spiral stairs

In the towers, see how the stone staircases wind up and around to the right. An enemy knight fighting his way up would hold his sword in his right hand and would have little space to use it properly.

8 The moat

Is there a dry, grassy ditch? Once, this would have been the moat—a deep trench filled with water to keep the enemy at a distance.

Invasion

After Edward I of England invaded Wales in 1277, he built eight new castles around the coast. Five of these castles had fortified towns built with them. One of the best known of these castle towns is Conwy, which was begun in 1283 and was completed in just four years.

Fire!

In 1401 Conwy town was burned down by the Welsh, but the castle and town walls still stand today.

A CASTLE TOWN

 Many towns in the Middle Ages were protected by a castle. Sometimes the castle was built long after the town had grown up. Sometimes the town grew up around an existing castle's walls. In newly-conquered lands, however, a castle and town were usually planned as one unit, and their walls were put up at the same time. These new towns were often settled by people who were loyal to the castle's lord.

The town of Conwy

1 harbor
2 lower gate
3 postern gate
4 Conwy Castle
5 Castle Street
6 St. Mary's Church
7 Llywelyn's Hall
8 water mill
9 High Street
10 market square
11 mill gate
12 Rosemary Lane
13 wall walk (This ran all the way around the town.)
14 Upper Gate Street
15 upper gate
16 gang of workers painting the town walls white

Master mason

Edward I hired the greatest castle-builder in Europe, Master James of St. George from Savoy (now part of France). Master James was responsible for building all of Edward's castles in North Wales. He designed Conwy Castle so that its massive walls formed part of the town's own wall defenses.

▲ Important towns had their own seal. Conwy's seal, pictured here, dates from about 1320.

Gates and walls

In times of trouble, the gatehouse of a castle town would have been well guarded, with soldiers on sentry duty day and night. The sentries were usually real busybodies, searching carts and baskets and asking strangers awkward questions. Traders on their way to market probably had to slip the guards a bribe—a jug of ale, a pie, or perhaps a silver coin, and an unwelcome visitor could expect an arrow in the throat.

◀ **The coat of arms of the City of Lancaster, England.**

▲ **London was ringed by defensive walls and was protected by the Tower of London (the White Tower).**

Curfew hour
At night, a bell was rung and the doors of the town were shut and barred. No one could then enter or leave until daybreak. The bell was also the signal for the townsfolk to cover their fires with dome-shaped clay pots before going to bed. The pots were called curfews (from the French word *couvrefeu*, meaning to cover fire).

Independence
Many castle towns displayed the lord's badge or coat of arms above their gates. Some towns, however, had their own coat of arms to show that the townsfolk did not live under the shadow of a castle or lord. The townspeople paid the lord rent in return for their freedom. These towns were usually fortified with high walls, gatehouses, and even a small army.

A great city
In the early 1300s London had about 80,000 people, and was one of the largest towns in Europe. Other towns were usually much smaller, with under 2,000 people.

▶ **As there wasn't enough land inside a town's walls for growing crops or keeping animals, the townsfolk had to buy food from local farmers.**

Town defenses

In times of trouble, an enemy attacker would have to get through the town's defenses before reaching the castle itself. As towns had exactly the same kind of defenses as the castle, this was no easy task. Armed soldiers protected the town's long wall walks, and the gate-houses could be sealed off by heavy, timber-framed portcullises, studded with iron. The soldiers fired arrows through narrow slits built into the walls. These slits were called loops.

15

Town houses

Many town houses had wooden frames. The spaces between the timbers were filled with wattle and daub—criss-crossed sticks plastered with clay (1).

Market day

 Most castle towns held a market once or twice a week. On market day the town square would be filled with bustling crowds and traders shouting their wares. Visitors could buy anything from candles, shoes, and knives to a refreshing draft ale. A couple of times a year there was also a fair that was bigger than a market and sold many more goods.

Street signs

Few people could read, so special signs were hung outside stores so that people knew what was being sold. For example, a horseshoe hung outside a farrier's, and a green bush was the sign for an inn.

Learning a trade

Many young boys in the town became apprentices. They were sent to live with the family of a master craftsman and learned his skills. After seven years they were free to leave and set up on their own.

► A cooper taught his apprentice the craft of barrel-making.

Muddy streets

Streets were very muddy and dirty. There were no proper drains, just open ditches where water and garbage collected (2). They were also very smelly— waste was simply thrown out of the windows!

Goods for sale

Goods produced locally, such as pottery (3), purses, and belts (4), were sold by the artisans who made them. Luxury items, such as finely woven cloth (5) or decorated jugs and bowls from Italy (6), were brought to market by merchants.

In many towns artisans and merchants belonged to societies called guilds. The guild controlled prices, organized training, and made sure that goods were of a high standard. Often, artisans' workshops were found in one street or area of a town. Some town streets still carry the name of the traders who worked there, such as Threadneedle Street or Ironmongers Lane.

Entertainers

Even if you couldn't afford the fine goods for sale, it cost only a farthing or halfpenny to watch stilt-walkers and jugglers (7) or perhaps a dancing bear (8).

Moneylenders

Nobles and even kings sometimes needed to borrow money to pay artisans or fight wars. Some moneylenders, therefore, became very rich.

► When coins became worn out, they were bought by weight.

1 Hourds

Wooden hourds were fitted to the battlements. Gaps in the floor of the hourds allowed soldiers to drop missiles onto the heads of anyone below.

2 Battlements

The tops of the walls had solid parts called merlons, which helped to shelter the defenders during an enemy attack. The defenders could fire through gaps called crenels, which had wooden shutters for extra protection.

3 Drawbridge

The wooden drawbridge could swing up like a seesaw so that no one could cross the ditch.

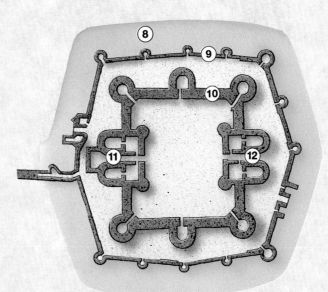

7 Tower defenses
In case the enemy used flaming arrows to set fire to the timber defenses, wooden hourds were made fireproof by stretching damp hides across their roofs.

6 Machicolations
These were stone versions of the wooden hourds. The battlements projected outward so that missiles could be dropped through overhanging chutes.

CASTLE DEFENSES

Many castles were built on high ground with clear views of the surrounding countryside—making a surprise attack out of the question. As an enemy attacker neared the castle, its massive walls and towers would loom menacingly above him. The only entrance was through a terrifying outer gatehouse, behind which was a barbican protecting the inner gate. Even if an attacker broke through this set of defenses, there were more gates, walls, and towers to overcome before the castle could be captured.

4 Portcullis
The portcullis slid down grooves in the stone walls. It was fixed to ropes and was operated by winding gear in the upper part of the gatehouse.

5 The barbican
The barbican was a walled area in front of the inner gatehouse. If an enemy reached it, he would be fired at from all sides by the castle defenders.

Beaumaris Castle
Beaumaris Castle in Wales was designed so that there were no weak points. This plan shows its moat (8), outer walls (9), inner walls (10), and two huge gatehouses (11 and 12). Building began in 1295 but was never completed.

Warriors and arms

 In peacetime a castle was guarded by just a small garrison of men. A typical garrison had about 12 soldiers armed with longbows and crossbows. Sometimes, local men who owed their lord military service would also be put on guard duty. They were usually poorly equipped, so the castle armorer had to make sure that there was always a ready supply of weapons, bowstrings, and arrows.

Fighting men

Ordinary soldiers fought on foot. They were protected by a simple padded tunic or by bits of armor they had found on the battlefield. Most fought with a knife, a halberd (a blade fixed to a long pole), or perhaps a sword. The knights, on the other hand, could afford to be better equipped. A knight's sword, horse, and armor could cost as much as a peasant's lifetime wages!

halberd

Lance and sword

In battle a knight used a lance to knock his enemies off their horses. But his most treasured possession was his sword.

In times of war a king would call on his lords and their knights to fight. Each knight had to provide his own armor and warhorse. Kings often hired mercenaries—professional soldiers who did not owe loyalty to a particular lord—to make up a strong fighting force.

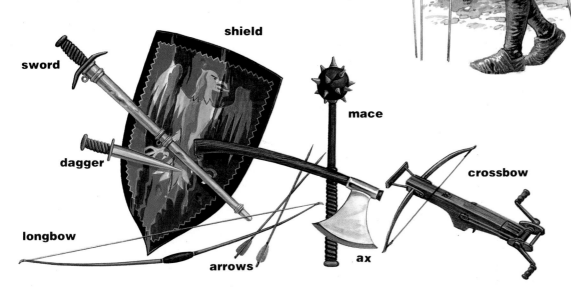

sword

dagger

shield

longbow

arrows

mace

ax

crossbow

Deadly weapons

The most frightening sound in battle was the hissing flight of steel-tipped arrows. A skilled longbowman could hit a target up to 300 feet away and fire up to 12 arrows a minute. Crossbows were even more accurate but were slower to load.

▼ Loading a crossbow

◄ This scene shows a oastle under attack from crossbowmen and knights.

Becoming a knight

Knights were the most important fighting men in the Middle Ages. The first knights appeared in the 700s after a new invention arrived in Europe from Asia. This was the stirrup—a footrest which helped mounted soldiers fight in the saddle and charge the enemy. Soon, cavalry became the most important part of an army, and knights became more and more powerful off the battlefield.

The knight's vigil

The evening before becoming a knight, a young man was bathed and shaved. Esquires dressed him in simple robes and he was led to the chapel, where he spent the night in prayer.

▶ The young men were expected to pray for guidance on how to be good knights.

Dubbing a knight

His nighttime vigil over, the young man got dressed in his finest clothes and went to the great hall, where his family and friends would be waiting to greet him. After breakfast, the ceremony called dubbing took place. The lord lightly tapped the young man with a sword, then gave him a sharp blow with the hand. The young knight was then presented with his own sword and spurs—usually a gift from his father or the lord himself. Finally, the newly-made knight returned to the chapel for a blessing by the priest.

▲ The page served in the great hall. From this he learned good manners.

▲ He spent long hours practicing swordplay, using a wooden sword.

▲ An esquire helped his knight prepare for battle.

► If an esquire had been especially brave in battle, he was knighted on the battlefield.

From page . . .

At the age of seven a boy who was going to be a knight went to live with another noble family as their page. He served at meals, helped the lord dress in the morning, and learned how to ride and fight with a sword.

. . . to knight

At the age of 14 the page became a knight's esquire. He was expected to follow his master into battle and look after his horses and armor. Most esquires had become knights by the time they were 21 years old.

Fighting monks

There were knights who were also monks. The Knights Hospitaller looked after the sick, and the Knights Templar were formed to protect pilgrims who visited the Holy Land. During the Crusades, both groups fought fiercely against the Saracens.

◄ Knights Templar (left) and Knights Hospitaller (right) followed strict religious rules.

There was more to knighthood than fighting—there was also chivalry. At first this word just meant horsemanship, but by the 1100s it had also come to mean a whole way of life. Knights were expected to be honorable and brave, to protect the weak, and to respect women. Tales of ancient chivalry became very popular during the Middle Ages, but even so, many knights failed to live up to these high standards.

The armor diagram is labeled as follows:

- helmet
- bevor
- breastplate
- pauldron
- besagew
- vambrace
- cuisse
- greave
- sabaton
- gauntlet
- tasset

The story of armor

The first knights were protected by a hauberk. Over the top they wore a surcoat which stopped them from getting too hot in the sun. The hauberk was made of chain mail—hundreds of small metal rings which had been linked together. In the 1300s, mail coats became shorter and solid plates of armor were added to protect the chest, knees, thighs, and arms. By the 1420s, the whole body was covered by a suit of plate armor.

Armorers' marks

Some of the best armor came from towns in present-day Germany. When a suit of plate armor was finished, it was stamped with the town's own special mark.

Augsburg   **Solingen and Passau**

◄ Plate armor was made from silvery steel. It was sometimes called white armor.

1100s

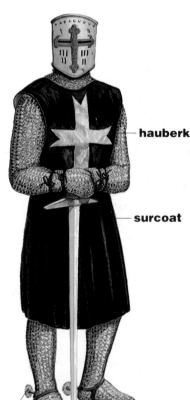

- hauberk
- surcoat
- spur

Chain mail

Making chain mail was a highly skilled craft. Thick iron wire was bent around a rod and then chopped into an open ring. The ends were hammered flat and pierced with tiny holes. Then the rings were then linked together and the ends bent around until the holes overlapped. Finally, they were joined with an iron rivet. It was a bit like knitting—in iron!

rivet

ring

linked mail

1300s

bascinet

coif

1400s

Dressing up

It could take up to an hour for a knight to dress for battle. He put on padded underclothes while his esquire brought out the armor. The leg armor (1) was strapped on or laced to the belt. The breastplate (2) and backplate came next, followed by the pauldrons and vambraces (3). Then the gauntlets went on and finally the helmet (4).

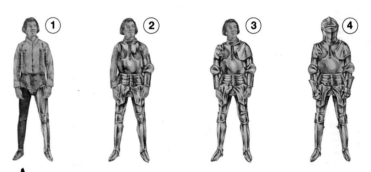

① ② ③ ④

A suit of plate armor weighed about 40 to 55 pounds. Even though it looked difficult to move around in, it was actually quite flexible, and a knight could easily maneuver in battle. Plate armor offered much more protection than chain mail against the cuts and blows of a sword or mace. But it was still no defense against the lethal power of a steel-tipped crossbow bolt or a well-aimed longbow shaft.

Food and drink

Most castles kept only a small amount of food in storage all year round. But when the king or lord visited, the courtyard would ring with commands and curses and the clatter of rolling barrels. Servants filled the cellars and storerooms with sides of salty bacon and heavy sacks of grain and flour. The steward would check old supplies to make sure that the grain for making bread had not gone moldy, or the wine had not turned sour.

barley

rye

wheat

Daily bread

Before it could be made into bread, grain such as barley, rye, and wheat had to be ground into flour. Some castles had their own windmills which were built high on the castle or town walls. There, the windmill's sails would catch the wind and turn the heavy grinding stones inside.

Preserving food

Although a castle's stone cellars were cool, it was impossible to keep food fresh for long. Most meat was therefore smoked or heavily salted so that it would last through the winter. Vegetables were dried or pickled.

Sometimes, layers of fruit and meat were stored together in barrels. The fruit juices soaked into the meat and helped to preserve it.

Mushrooms and onions (1) were often threaded on long strings and hung up to dry.

Most large castles had a pantler (5), who looked after the food supplies stored in the pantry (from the French word *painetterie*, meaning bread store).

Castle residents

While the lord was away, the constable was put in charge of the castle. He was a knight and often one of the lord's relatives. The constable appointed other castle officials, such as the steward, who looked after the castle's finances and supplies.

Castle visitors

The lord brought a huge household with him, perhaps swelling the number of residents from 20 to 200! His household would include a priest, soldiers, and a host of servants. Fellow lords also came to stay. There were entertainers too—jugglers, jesters, minstrels, and traveling actors called mummers.

While the lord was in residence, he inspected his lands, met his castle officials to make sure that everything had been running smoothly, passed judgment on prisoners, and entertained his guests with hunting, feasting, and perhaps a joust. A lord with several castles spent only a few months a year at each. The rest of the time he might be at the king's court or fighting overseas.

Key

1 watergate
2 east barbican
3 chapel tower
4 king's tower
5 king's chamber
6 storeroom
7 well
8 pentice
9 kitchen tower
10 kitchen
11 great hall
12 prison tower
13 garderobe
14 northwest tower
15 southwest tower
16 west barbican
17 gatehouse
18 town wall

Plan of Conwy Castle

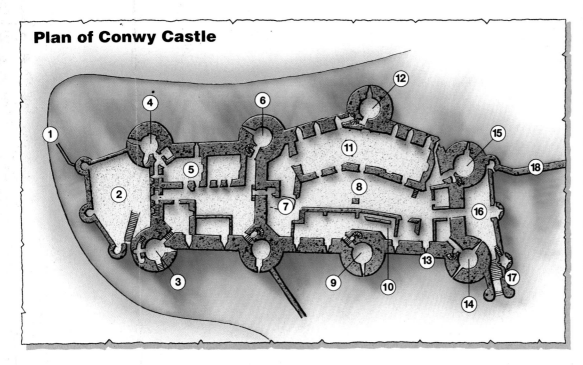

Fire hazard

Due to the danger of fire, the kitchen had its own separate building in the courtyard. It was usually connected to the great hall by a covered passageway called a pentice. Because of the distance it had to be carried, food was often stone cold by the time it reached the table!

Out of sight

Conwy Castle had its own prison at the bottom of the prison tower. In most castles, prisoners were usually locked up in cellars. Some prisons were called *oubliettes*, from the French word *oublier*, meaning to forget.

▼ At castles built next to rivers or the sea, visitors could arrive by boat at a special entrance called a watergate.

◄ Many castles had their own well-tended garden for growing herbs and vegetables. The garden at Conwy Castle was in the east barbican.

CASTLE LIFE

In times of peace only a few soldiers were needed to patrol the castle walls, and the hourds were taken down from the battlements. The castle was quiet for much of the year, but when the lord arrived for one of his visits or the king came to stay, the castle was filled with the hustle and bustle of everyday life.

White meats

Milk from sheep, goats, and cows, and the cream, butter, and cheese made from it were called white meats. The creamiest part of the milk was made into soft cheese or butter for the lord

and his family. Servants had to make do with a thick, hard cheese made from the rest of the milk. Sometimes this cheese was so tough it had to be smashed into pieces with a hammer before it could be eaten!

Meat was salted in a salting box (2). Then it was hung on huge hooks (3) or stored in barrels (4).

Well water

Every castle needed its own supply of fresh water—especially if it was to survive a siege. Deep stone-lined shafts were dug to underground springs, and the water was raised in wooden buckets using a rope and a windlass. Sometimes water was channeled straight to the kitchens.

Special jobs

Some jobs carried great honor and importance. The butler looked after the castle's supplies of wine, and the ewerer made sure that the lord's tablecloths and napkins were always clean. Both these jobs were done by noblemen who were chosen by the lord.

ewerer

butler

As sweet as honey

Some castles kept honey bees. Honey was used to sweeten food and drink. It was also one of the main ingredients in mead—a strong alcoholic drink popular during the Middle Ages.

Larger castles had their own fishponds, orchards, and vineyards, as well as gardens which supplied vegetables and herbs. Cattle, sheep, and pigs were kept on surrounding farmlands. The lord's hunting parties also brought back deer, wild boar, and pheasants from the forests for special feasts.

The kitchen

When the lord was away, the castle kitchen was quiet. The constable might eat alone in his private room, and a small garrison needed only basic meals. However, during the lord's visit the kitchen buzzed with activity. The cook bellowed orders, and the under-cooks chopped vegetables, plucked poultry, and pounded meat until it was tender. The worst jobs in the kitchen, such as cleaning the cauldron or fetching water from the well, were done by young boys called scullions.

adjustable pot-hook

Cauldron cooking

All kitchens had at least one big iron cauldron which was slung on a hook over an open fire. Cauldrons were used for stews, soups, and sauces. Sometimes they were packed with several dishes, all to be cooked at once—shown here: eggs (1), chickens (2), and fish (3), in sealed pottery jars, puddings in cloth bags (4), and a slab of bacon (5).

Spice it up

Food was often heavily spiced, which helped to disguise the taste of rotten meat! Many spices came from the Middle and Far East. They were very expensive, so only the rich could afford them.

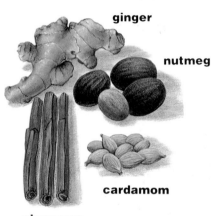

ginger

nutmeg

cardamom

cinnamon

▼ Pots and plates were cleaned with sand or with soapy herbs like soapwort. Dirty water was poured away through a sink built into an outside wall.

Kitchen tools

Important kitchen tools included a pestle and mortar (1) for grinding up spices and herbs, a stirring stick (2), a meat pounder (3), a metal skimmer for soups (4), and various knives for chopping up vegetables and meat (5).

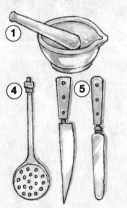

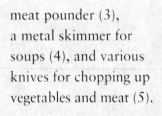

The warmest part of the kitchen was in front of the blazing hearth. Here, a scullion called a turnspit had the hot and sweaty job of turning a long pole on which meat was skewered for roasting. A dome-shaped oven for baking bread was usually built into the side of the hearth. It was heated with blazing brushwood and stayed hot for hours.

Multi-colored food
Food was not only spicy, it was also colored with vegetable dyes and sometimes gilded with gold. Parsley was used for green, saffron for yellow, and sandalwood for red.

The great hall

On special occasions magnificent banquets were held in the castle's great hall. The lord, his family, and the most important guests sat at the high table, which was raised above the other diners and covered with a tablecloth of the finest linen. A gold or silver boat-shaped ornament called a nef was placed in the middle of the table and was used to hold the lord's napkin.

► The cup-bearer stood to the left of the lord. He made sure that the lord's cup was always filled with wine.

Table manners
There were rules about how to behave when eating meals. Just like today, it was thought rude to talk with your mouth full or to munch noisily as you ate.

◄ Some lords didn't care much about fine table manners!

After a fanfare of trumpets sounded, a procession of servants brought in the dishes. Guests might be offered soups and aspics; eels and lampreys; roast goose, heron, or swan; huge pies; and fruit tarts. The food was served up in dishes called messes which were shared between several people. Honored guests had their own messes and ate off gold or silver plates. Everyone else used a trencher—a big slice of stale bread which soaked up the grease from the food. Leftovers were saved for the poor waiting at the castle gates.

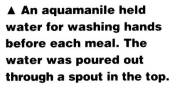

▲ An aquamanile held water for washing hands before each meal. The water was poured out through a spout in the top.

An early start

Banquets and other formal meals began early— at about 10 or 11 in the morning—and lasted for several hours.

Polite company

Guests with good manners would share cups of wine and offer food from their own plates to a neighbor.

Guests ate with their fingers or with knives or spoons. Forks were not used until the end of the Middle Ages.

▶ Food that was soft and mushy could be scooped up onto bread. Other foods were carved into small pieces that could be picked up with a knife.

Home life

In early castles, life was far from comfortable. The wind whistled through wooden shutters in the windows, and most people slept on benches or on rough mattresses in the great hall. By the 1200s, castles had well-furnished bed chambers and living rooms heated by large open fires and lit by candles. The better rooms had glass windows and plastered walls hung with fine tapestries. Floors were covered with sweet-smelling herbs or rush matting.

1 The wardrobe
The top room in the lord's tower was used by the lady's personal servants. Linen and clothes were stored in large chests.

2 Master bedroom
This had rush mats on the floor and richly decorated walls. A lady-in-waiting could sleep on the trundle bed, which was pulled out from under the main bed.

3 The solar
This was the lord's private living room. After a hearty meal he might retire here for a game of chess.

4 Basement
A trapdoor from the solar led down to the basement. Weapons, coins, and other valuables might have been kept here.

Reading and writing

Few people in the Middle Ages knew how to read and write. There were not many schools, and most children never went to one. Boys had more opportunity to learn than girls, but there were still some famous women writers, such as Christine de Pisan, who lived in France in the 1400s.

Entertainment

Traveling musicians called jongleurs often visited the castle to entertain guests. Lords and ladies also liked to play music, sing, and compose poetry themselves. Listening to storytellers' tales of romance and chivalry, embroidering, and playing chess were other popular pastimes.

harpist

lute player

The lady, the wife of the lord, usually played an important part in running the castle. She organized the servants and entertained visiting noblewomen. When the lord was away, she might inspect local farms or manage supplies and repairs to the castle. Even so, this was still a man's world. It was believed that women were inferior to men. In some places, they could not own land or make a will.

Marrying young

Marriages between nobles were arranged when the children were still in their cradles. Most lords and ladies were married by the time they were fourteen.

Growing up

From the age of six or seven, the children of nobles were often sent to live in another lord's castle. Boys became pages and learned how to fight. Girls learned how to manage a household.

Clean and healthy

People in the Middle Ages were much less fussy about living in smelly and dirty places than we are today. A castle's toilets were little more than holes with stone seats, few rooms had running water, and baths were an expensive luxury. Every now and then the castle was cleaned from top to bottom. Wisely, the lord and lady would leave for a week or two while the whole building was aired, scrubbed, and swept. The horrible job of cleaning out the cesspits below the toilets was done by men called gong farmers.

▶ Toilets were sometimes built on different floors, one above the other. The topmost one was often in the open air.

▲ A green baize cloth with a hole cut in the middle helped warm up the cold stone seat.

▼ Waste from the garderobes dropped down into the moat or into a special pit.

Garderobes

The lord sometimes had his own private toilet, or garderobe, next to his chambers. Torn strips of linen were used instead of toilet paper, and sweet-smelling herbs were sprinkled on the floor.

Rats, rats, rats

Rats were everywhere—in the kitchens, in the cellars, in the stables... Rats destroyed stores of grain and spread diseases. They carried the fleas which spread the deadly sickness called the plague.

Bathtime

Only the richest people could enjoy a soak in a hot bath. Wood for heating the water, cloth to line the tub, and bath oils all had to be paid for. King John of England bathed once a month, and it cost him five pence each time. (A laborer had to work a whole week to earn this amount.)

40

Herbal remedies

In the Middle Ages, doctors often used herbs to treat their patients. Comfrey was meant to help broken bones mend quickly. Yarrow was applied to flesh wounds to help stop any bleeding.

Between 1347 and 1351 a plague known as the Black Death killed about 25 million people in Europe and Asia. People knew nothing about the germs that spread disease. Young women died giving birth, and young men died of wounds they received in battle. But if people escaped these disasters, they often lived to a ripe old age.

▼ Apart from ladies-in-waiting, laundresses were the only other women who worked in the castle. The rest of the jobs were done by men and boys.

Making soap

Soap made from olive oil and scented with herbs was used in southern Europe from the 700s but was not widely available in northern Europe until much later. Often, soap was made locally from animal fat, wood ash, and soda.

► Folded clothes and bedding were put into a barrel, and liquid soap was poured through them. Then they were pounded with a wooden bat to remove the dirt.

41

Keeping in fashion

Fashion was very important in the Middle Ages. Just as kings built huge castles to impress people, the wealthy dressed in rich costumes to impress each other. On important occasions noblemen and noblewomen wore jewels, gold chains, and brightly colored clothes. Colors had different meanings. Blue meant you were in love, yellow meant anger, and gray meant sadness.

◄ Women often hid their hair beneath head-dresses. Some of these were shaped like animal horns and others like butterflies' wings.

► The steeple hat, or hennin, could be nearly three feet tall! It needed a wire frame inside to support it.

▼ Some men's shoes were so pointed that the toes had to be tied back. Others had wooden platforms for walking through muddy streets.

Trendsetters

In the early 1400s, the well-dressed nobleman might wear a hat with a tail called a liripipe, which draped over his shoulder (1). In the 1450s, knee-length clothes trimmed with fur (2) became popular with the nobles, while merchants wore longer robes (3). Women's dresses often had long trains, which were looped over the arm (4), and hats were very tall (5). Short tunics and pointed shoes (6) were all the rage with the most fashionable young men.

Working clothes

Peasants could not afford to buy fancy clothes. Instead, they wore simple tunics and shifts, wool stockings, cloaks, straw hats, hoods, and caps. With frequent repairing, these clothes could last for many years.

▼ There were no stores selling ready-made clothes, so the rich paid tailors to make the latest fashions.

In the early Middle Ages, the rich wore fairly simple clothes. But from the 1100s, fashions became more and more elaborate. Just like today, fashions such as hats, shoes, hairstyles, tunics, and coats varied from time to time. Laws banning outrageous dress were passed in many parts of Europe in the 1200s and 1300s— but they were usually ignored.

The chapel

Most castles had a small private chapel near the lord's chambers. Painted walls, stained glass windows, and a golden cross on the altar made it the castle's most beautiful room. The lord and lady began each day by attending a short service here.

Some castles also had a larger chapel in the courtyard for the other castle residents.

▲ Bibles and other books were handwritten and richly decorated.

Prayer time

Religious ceremonies in the castle's chapel were performed by the priest. He also said grace before the beginning of every meal, thanking God for the food about to be eaten. Priests were among the few people in the castle who could read and write. They were often put in charge of castle documents.

Holy days

Religious festivals were an important part of everyday life. They were celebrated with public holidays, when everybody took the day off work. Sometimes, traveling actors performed mystery and miracle plays in front of a church or cathedral. These showed well-known stories from the Bible or the lives of saints.

▶ **Other entertainers often tried to lure away a play's audience!**

▼ **Pilgrims who had been to Santiago de Compostela wore cockleshells in their hats.**

▼ **Dishonest relic sellers sold wooden crosses, which they claimed were made from the cross on which Jesus was crucified.**

relic seller

nun

pilgrim

bishop   monk

During the Middle Ages most people were very religious. Many Christians proved their faith by going on pilgrimages. They traveled huge distances to visit holy places such as Rome, Jerusalem, and Santiago de Compostela in Spain. Others became monks or nuns and lived in abbeys, monasteries, or convents. Here, they spent their lives in prayer, copying out the scriptures, or helping the sick.

Hunting and hawking

The best-loved sport was hunting, and most lords kept special horses for tracking game. The horses were well cared for and often led a better life than the servants who looked after them! Hunting dogs were also highly valued. They were specially trained to sniff out and track down their prey. Nearly every king and lord had a favorite hound which followed him around the castle. The dogs were looked after by the lord's huntsmen and kennel-grooms.

The hunt

Some of the animals hunted by the nobles included deer, wild boar, wolves, foxes, and bears. Hunting was more than a sport—it also provided meat for the dinner table.

▲ This scene shows a pack of hunting dogs catching a wild boar. Dogs wore collars to protect their throats in case the boar tried to gore them with its sharp tusks.

Falconry

Birds of prey were the most prized of all hunting animals. It took time and great skill to train them to catch smaller birds, hares, and rabbits. The type of bird you hunted with depended on your rank in society. An emperor hunted with an eagle, a king or queen with a gyrfalcon, a lord with a peregrine falcon, and a noblewoman with a hawk. Birds of prey were kept in a long wooden shed called a mews and were looked after by the falconer.

▶ **A falconer wore a gauntlet to protect his hand from the bird's sharp claws.**

In the early Middle Ages, Europe had huge forests which teemed with deer, wild boar, foxes, and bears. But over the years, large areas of woodland were cut down and turned into farmland. By the 1100s, some areas were set aside just for hunting. These were called royal forests, and any peasants found poaching game from them faced harsh punishment. If they were caught they might be blinded or even killed, but many still tried to catch a hare or squirrel for the pot.

Falconry kit

Special equipment was used to train and look after birds of prey. A leash stopped a bird from flying away, bells helped to find a lost bird, a hood kept it calm, and a leather purse might contain a tasty reward.

leash

bells

hood

purse

The joust

War games were popular in the Middle Ages. Mock battles, called tournaments, involving hundreds of men were held in huge open fields. They started as a way of training knights for battle. Later, they were used to settle disputes. The contestants fought with real weapons, and the loser had to give the winner money or horses. In the 1200s, tournaments became spectacular festivals—and a chance for the knights to show off.

jousting spur

► In the joust, two knights armed with wooden lances charged toward each other.

All for a lady

Tournaments were meant to be displays of bravery and honor, and any knight who behaved in an unchivalrous way was disgraced. A lady would tie a scarf to the arm of a favored knight.

Broken ends

Unhorsing an opponent was only one way of winning a joust. Points were also scored for breaking the end of your lance on an opponent's shield. The metal tips of the lances were usually blunt to make them less dangerous.

The tilt

In the 1400s, jousting knights were separated by a long fence called a tilt to stop them from crashing into each other. The field where the jousts were held became known as the tiltyard.

Practice makes perfect

An esquire would spend long hours practicing for the joust. He would charge at a quintain—a swiveling shield set up as a target. When the target was hit off center a heavy sack swung around. He needed quick reactions if he didn't want to be knocked off his horse!

► Practice at the quintain could help make an esquire a famous jouster one day.

The most exciting contest was the joust—a head-on clash between two knights on horseback. The aim was to knock your opponent off his horse with a wooden lance. Jousting armor was heavier and stronger than battle armor, and horses were protected with straw padding. Even so, injuries and deaths were common.

Field sports

Other games could be almost as violent as jousting. Many people were injured playing bandyball, an early kind of hockey. In England in the late 1300s, it was banned because it interfered with war training.

Heraldry

In the heat of battle, knowing your friend from your foe could mean the difference between life and death. But this wasn't so easy when a knight was covered from head to toe in armor! In order to be recognized, each knight decorated his shield and tunic with a special badge. The system used to design these badges is called heraldry.

Coat of arms

A surcoat decorated with a knight's badge, or charge, became known as a coat of arms. We now use this term to describe the badges themselves.

Shield designs

The most basic charges (top row) are called ordinaires. They can be divided (second row) or sub-divided (third row), and their edges can be patterned (bottom row).

chief	fesse	pale	bend	cross
per fesse	per pale	per bend	per cross	per saltire
barry	paly	bendy	checky	gyronny
per pale indented	barry wavy	bend raguly	chief embattled	cross engrailed

▼ In heraldry, every part of a shield has a special name.

in chief (top)

dexter (right side)

sinister (left side)

charge

field (background color)

in base (bottom)

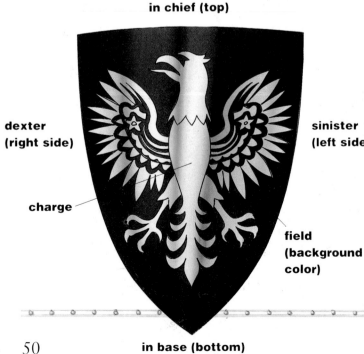

Heraldic colors

The colors used in heraldry include two metals—argent (silver) and or (gold)—and five main tinctures. The tinctures include azure (blue), gules (red), sable (black), vert (green), and purpure (purple). A metal charge must always be placed on a tincture field, and vice versa.

Impaling arms

Sometimes, the coats of arms of two families were combined to create a new coat of arms. This was called impaling, and it usually happened when a lord did not have any sons.

1 The coat of arms of a lord with no son.

2 His daughter marries into a family with this coat of arms.

3 The two coats of arms are combined.

4 When the lady's father dies, the coat of arms changes once again.

5 The lord and lady have a son. When the lord dies, the son has the coat of arms quartered, or divided into four.

Signs for sons

All family coats of arms have a different symbol for each member of the family. For example, the symbol for the second son is a crescent, or a new moon; for the third a mullet, or five-pointed star; for the fourth a martlet, or bird.

Heralds

The men who designed coats of arms were called heralds. They made sure that no two designs were the same, and they recorded them in books called armorials. Heralds also announced knights at tournaments.

In less peaceful times they made lists of the knights about to fight on the battlefield.

▼ After a battle was over a herald had the terrible task of identifying dead or dying knights by their coats of arms.

At first only lords and knights had coats of arms. They appeared on armor, flags, seals, and above the gatehouses of castles. These coats of arms were passed down from one generation to the next and showed that you came from an important family. Later in time, towns, guilds, and even important citizens could be granted a coat of arms.

Before settling down for a long siege, the commander might try to bribe the garrison to let him in, or to poison the castle's water supply.

The commander's troops would then surround the castle, burn down the homes of the local people, and cut off the castle's supply lines.

Wagons pulled by oxen would bring up the parts of the siege weapons so that they could be assembled nearer the castle walls.

A herald from the castle might come to discuss the terms of fighting.

BESIEGED!

 An enemy commander who wanted to capture a castle and the land around it had to plan his tactics carefully. Before beginning a siege he took a good look at the countryside. Could the castle be easily surrounded? Where were its weak spots? Where would the siege weapons be most effective?

▲ In 1370, the English besieged the town of Troyes in France. This picture from the 1470s shows English heralds asking the French to surrender.

If the castle could not be taken quickly, the attackers aimed to starve the castle's garrison until they had to give in. In fact, few castles held out to the bitter end. The constable might have to defend the castle for only 40 days. If his lord or his king had not sent help by then, the constable could surrender to the enemy with honor.

Under attack

The battle is now on. The enemy has assembled their siege weapons—the trebuchet and the mangonel—and has begun hurling boulders and flaming missiles at the defenses. The moat has been drained and filled with brushwood and earth. Soldiers clamber up a long scaling ladder thrown against the wall, and the belfry has reached the battlements. The defenders shelter behind the wooden hourds or take cover in the embrasures behind the arrow loops and return the enemy's fire.

1 Taking shelter
Crossbowmen and archers were protected from the castle defenders' fire by large wooden shields called pavises.

2 Filling the ditch
The ditch left after the moat had been drained was filled and boarded over so that the siege machines could be wheeled right up to the castle walls.

3 Battering ram
The soldiers pushing the battering ram against the castle gate were protected by a wooden frame covered in wet animal hides.

Undermining
Before castles had moats, or once a moat had been drained, the attackers could dig their way under the castle's walls. They then lit a fire in the tunnel so that the timbers supporting its roof collapsed, along with the walls above.

4 Belfry

The belfry tower allowed the attackers to make a direct assault on the battlements.

5 Trebuchet

This giant catapult was powered by a heavy counterweight. A sling at the other end hurled rocks against the walls.

6 Mangonel

The mangonel was another kind of catapult powered by twisted ropes.

7 Cannons

Cannon barrels were raised or lowered on a heavy wooden beam.

End of a siege

The weeks pass by slowly. The attackers are tiring, and the troops begin to mutter that they are wasting their time. If they haven't been able to batter down the walls, perhaps they can bribe their way in with offers of gold? The defenders have their own problems.

Food supplies are running out and water is strictly rationed. Then the defenders' luck changes—a lookout spies glinting armor in the distance. Help is less than a day's march away.

Cannon power

The first cannons were used in Europe during the early 1300s. They were poorly made and sometimes exploded in the faces of the gunners.

Over the years cannon design improved, but until the 1450s few were powerful enough to bring down a castle's walls.

▼ **The most powerful cannons were called bombards. Some were over 10 feet long.**

▲ When a castle or town was captured it was usually looted. Every soldier expected a share of the spoils.

No mercy

The attackers would have shown little mercy if they had managed to capture the castle before the defenders surrendered. Captured foot soldiers were often slaughtered by the victorious side. Knights were usually luckier. They could be held hostage until their friends or countrymen paid a large sum of money, called a ransom, for their release.

A band of defending knights and foot soldiers gather just behind a small door called the postein. Suddenly, the door bursts open and the soldiers pour out. Their main aim is to wreck the siege machines and kill the skilled men who work them. Taken by surprise, the enemy soldiers are now trapped—the relieving army is advancing behind them.

A king's ransom

Ransoms could be huge. In 1193, the Holy Roman Emperor, Henry VI, demanded 150,000 marks (about $23 million in today's money) for the release of Richard the Lionheart, King of England.

Castles in history

Castle design changed greatly over the ages. Simple wooden towers surrounded by fences and ditches gave way to massive stone castles ringed by walls and moats. Later castles were more like palaces, designed for comfortable living rather than for protection and controlling land.

Time line

476 End of the Roman Empire in Europe.

700s Introduction of stirrups to Europe from Asia helps horsemen fight from the saddle.

800s Feudalism develops in Western Europe.

950 Earliest known French castle built at Doué-la-Fontaine, Anjou.

1000s Chain mail armor worn by Normans.

stone keep

1066 William of Normandy invades England.

1080s Shell keeps built.

1096 Crusades begin.

1100s Stone keeps become the main castle stronghold. Crossbows and longbows in use.

1119 Order of Knights Templar founded.

1142 Crusaders take over Krak des Chevaliers in Syria.

motte

bailey

▲ 1000s
The first castles were made of wood. They stood on a mound called a motte. The outer enclosure was called a bailey.

▶ This map, drawn in 1497, shows some of the most important castles across the countries of Europe and North Africa.

1150—1250 Thousands of castles built across what is now Germany.

1180s Castles with square wall towers built.

1187 Jerusalem recaptured by Muslims.

1205 Krak des Chevaliers rebuilt by Knights Hospitaller.

1215 Signing of Magna Carta limits power of King of England.

◀ 1100s
Soon stone was being used to build a massive stronghold, or keep. This tower was the key to the whole castle's defense. Some keeps were square and some were round.

1220s Rounded wall towers begin to be built.

1270s Machicolations begin to replace wooden hourds.

1271 Krak des Chevaliers falls to Muslims.

1280s Edward I builds concentric castles in England and Wales.

1283 Conquest of Wales by Edward I.

1291 End of the Crusades.

1320s Cannons first used in battle.

1330 Plate armor in widespread use.

▼ 1290s
Concentric castles relied on rings of walls, towers, and strong gatehouses for their defense.

inner wall

outer wall

Castles around the world

▼ Saumur Castle in France was re-built several times during the Middle Ages.

Castles were built in many different styles. In France castles usually had tall pointed roofs on their towers. Spanish castles often had highly decorated stonework or brickwork, which showed the influence of the Moors. The main center of castle building outside Europe was Japan. Here, castles had overhanging roofs and wooden keeps built on stone basements.

▼ El Real de Manzanares in Spain was built as a castle-palace in 1475.

▲ Himeji Castle in Japan was home to Japanese knights called samurai.

1337 Start of Hundred Years' War between England and France.

1347–51 Black Death kills 25 million people across Europe.

1350s Some castles in Britain and Holland built from brick.

1400 Welsh rise against the English.

▲ **1400s**
Most European castles were no longer so heavily fortified. Herstmonceux in England had brick walls and large windows.

1400s Castle building declines in Europe.

1453 Constantinople falls to Turks, marking the end of the Middle Ages.

▶ **1800s**
The fairytale-like castle of Neuschwanstein was built for Ludwig II, the insane king of Bavaria.

Glossary

bailey The fenced enclosure of an early castle, later the courtyard and its surrounding walls.

banquet A great feast held in the great hall of a castle.

barbican A walled defense protecting a castle gatehouse from attack. A barbican could be either an outer enclosure or a narrow walled corridor.

bascinet A style of helmet with an ugly snout worn over the face.

bascinet

battering ram A huge beam of wood with a metal tip used for knocking down gates.

battlements The defensive parapets on top of castle walls.

belfry A siege tower.

besiege To surround a fort, castle, or town with an enemy army.

bolt A heavy, steel-tipped dart, about 15 inches long, fired from a crossbow. Its flights (vanes) were made of leather or wood. Also called a quarrel.

chivalry Knighthood and its code of honor. Stories about knights and how they should behave became popular from the 1200s.

coat of arms Any heraldic badge of the kind orginally displayed on a knight's surcoat but still used by towns and schools.

coif A round hood made of chain mail.

concentric castle A type of castle with two rings of defensive stone walls. Defenders on the higher inner walls could fire at the enemy over the lower outer walls.

concentric castle

constable A commander who looked after a castle while his lord was away. Sometimes known as a castellan.

crenels Gaps in the battlements for shooting arrows through.

crossbow A bow fixed to a wooden support which directed the bolt it fired. It could not be pulled by hand and needed rewinding after each shot.

Crusades A series of wars fought by Christians against Saracens for control of the Holy Land, the part of the Middle East where Jesus once lived. The first Crusade began in 1096 and the final one ended in 1291.

curfew 1) An order to remain inside a town or at home at night. 2) A clay dome-shaped pot used to cover fires.

Saracen warrior

drawbridge

drawbridge A bridge that can be drawn up or let down to prevent entry to a castle.

embrasure An opening built on the inner side of a loophole. It provided space for a defender when firing at the enemy.

empire A group of countries governed by a single ruler.

esquire A youth of over 14 who acted as the personal assistant of a knight. It comes from the French word *écuyer*, meaning shield-bearer. Also known as a squire.

farrier A person who shod horses and treated horses that were sick.

feudalism A system of agreements in which land was held in return for service or loyalty.

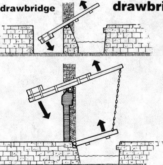
embrasure

fort A fortified military base.

garderobe A castle toilet. Also called the latrine or privy.

garrison The troops stationed in a castle or fort.

gatehouse The complex of towers and gates that guards the entrance of a town or castle.

gauntlet A protective glove used in fighting or hunting.

great hall The formal business room in a castle, also used for feasting.

guild An organization of skilled craftsmen or merchants.

halberd A sharp blade attached to a wooden pole. It could be used as a battle-ax or spear.

hauberk A long coat made of mail.

herald A designer of coats of arms. Also acted as an official at battles and tournaments.

heraldry The official system of drawing up coats of arms.

high table The most important table in the great hall.

hourd Movable wooden frame fitted onto the battlements to help defend the walls. Hourds were later replaced by permanent stone machicolations.

joust A contest in which one knight tries to knock the other off his horse.

keep A defensive stone tower at the center of a castle, also known as a donjon.

knight A warrior who fought on horseback. Kings and lords and some of the men who served them were knights.

lamprey A type of fish considered a great delicacy in the Middle Ages.

lance A long spear used by knights in battle and jousts.

longbow A bow made of yew wood about 6 feet long.

loophole An opening in a defensive wall through which weapons were fired. Some loops were simple vertical slits, others were shaped like crosses and had holes for guns.

gun hole

lord A member of the most powerful group in society. Nobles and the king himself were part of this group. The lord of a castle was its owner.

mace A metal club often fitted with spikes or chains.

machicolations Stone overhangs at the top of a tower or wall. The openings allowed defenders to drop boulders onto attackers down below or put out a fire with water.

machicolations

mail Carefully linked iron rings used as body armor.

mangonel A kind of giant catapult, used to knock down castle walls.

mason A worker in stone. Each mason had his own personal mark which he carved into the finished stone. These marks can still be seen on many castle walls.

merlon   crenel   shutter

master mason A person in charge of all the other masons on a building site.

merlon The raised wall between two crenels that gave cover to an archer.

mews Sheds used for falconry. A mew was the cage in which hawks were kept while molting (shedding feathers).

moat A water-filled ditch around a castle.

mortar 1) A mixture used to bind stones or bricks together. 2) A bowl used for grinding herbs and spices.

motte A steep earth mound that supported the towers of early castles.

murder hole Hole in a gatehouse ceiling, used either to drop missiles on attackers below, or to put out fires—somewhat like a modern sprinkler system.

nef A boat-shaped dish that held napkins and table knives.

oubliette A name sometimes given to a cellar where prisoners were kept and could be forgotten. It comes from the French word *oublier*, meaning to forget.

page A boy of noble birth, aged between 7 and 14, in training for knighthood.

pavise A body-sized shield or screen used to protect archers in battle.

peasant A country dweller who worked on the land.

pestle A stick or rod for grinding up herbs and spices.

pilgrimage A journey to the Holy Land or to a shrine.

plate armor Fitted body armor made from steel sections.

portcullis A heavy grille used to seal off a castle gateway.

postern A small door in a castle wall through which soldiers could leave and enter when the main gateway was not in use. Also known as the sallyport.

quarry A pit dug for the supply of stone or slate.

quintain A target post used by knights when they practiced charging. A heavy sack swung around when the target was hit.

scullion A very junior servant who worked in the kitchen.

sentry A soldier who guarded a gate or bridge.

shell keep A defensive stone wall that replaced the wooden fence on top of a motte.

spurs

siege Cutting off a castle by an enemy army.

solar A large living room inside a castle tower.

spur A point fitted to a rider's heel, worn to make the horse go faster. Spurs were a badge of knighthood.

stirrup A loop hung from a horse's saddle, designed to support the rider's foot.

surcoat A loose tunic worn over armor.

tapestry A woven wall hanging.

tilt A fence separating two jousting knights.

murder holes

tournament Fighting staged as a series of sporting events. A great festival was held which could last up to a week.

portcullis

trebuchet A siege machine used for hurling rocks against a castle's walls. Sometimes dead animals were also thrown over the walls to spread disease.

trencher Originally, a slice of stale bread used as a plate or dish-liner. Later the word was used to mean a plate made of wood or metal.

undermining Digging underneath the walls of a castle to make them fall down.

wardrobe A small room, usually next to the lord's bedroom, for storing clothes and working out household accounts.

watergate A small gate leading directly to a river or the sea.

shell keep

wattle and daub A mixture of wood, clay, straw, and animal hair used in the construction of timber buildings.

Index

A
apprentice 17
aquamanile 37
armorial 51
armor, making 25
  putting on 25
  types of 24–25, 49
armorer 20
armorer's marks 24
arrow-loops 15
  see also loopholes
ax, battle 21
  carpenter's 9
  mason's 9

B
bailey 58, 60
bandyball 49
banquet 36, 60
barbican 19, 60

bascinet 25, 60
bathing 40
battering ram 54
battlements 18, 19, 26, 60
Beaumaris Castle 9, 19
bedrooms 38
belfry 54, 55, 60
bird of prey 47
Black Death 41, 59
blacksmith 7, 8, 9
bolt, crossbow 60
bombard 56
bread 32, 35
building castles 8–9
butler 33

C
cannons 55, 56, 58
carpenter 8, 9,
cathedral 7, 45
cauldron 34
cellars 27, 32
chain mail 24, 25, 58, 61
chapel 7, 11, 22, 44
chess 38, 39
children 39
chivalry 23, 39, 48, 60
Christianity 7, 45
clothes 42–43
coat of arms 14, 50–51, 60
coif 25, 60
concentric castle 58, 60
constable 30, 34, 53, 60
Conwy Castle 12, 13, 27
cook 34
cooper 17
craftsman 7, 17
crenel 18, 60
crossbow 20, 21, 25, 60
Crusades 4, 23, 58, 60
cup-bearer 36
curfew 14, 60

D
deer 33, 46, 47
defense 18–19
disease 40, 41
drawbridge 18, 60
dubbing a knight 22

E
Edward I, King 12, 13, 58
embrasure 54, 60
entertainment 17, 30, 39

esquire 22, 23, 25, 49, 60
ewerer 33

F
fair 16
falconry 47
farrier 17, 60
feasting 27, 36–37
feudal system 6, 58, 60
fireplace 11, 35
food 32, 33, 34–35, 36–37
  preserving 32
freemason 8

G
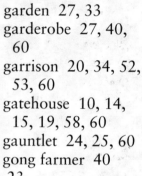

garden 27, 33
garderobe 27, 40, 60
garrison 20, 34, 52, 53, 60
gatehouse 10, 14, 15, 19, 58, 60
gauntlet 24, 25, 60
gong farmer 40
great hall 22, 23, 27, 36–37, 38, 60
guild 17, 51, 60

H
halberd 20, 60
hauberk 24, 60
hawking 47
hennin 42
herald 51, 52, 53, 60
heraldry 50–51, 60
herbs 34, 38, 40, 41
Herstmonceux Castle 59
high table 36, 60
Himeji Castle 59
horse 46, 49
hostage 57
hound 46
hourd 11, 18, 19, 26, 54, 58, 60
household 30, 39
hunting 27, 33, 46–47

J
jester 30
John, King 6, 7, 40
jongleur 39
jousting 27, 48–49, 60

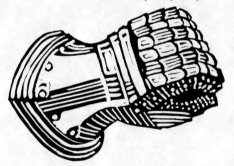
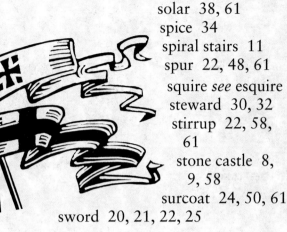

Acknowledgments

The publishers would like to thank the following
illustrators for their contribution to this book:

Julian Baker 9*r*, 17*tl*, 19*r*, 21*c*, 24, 25*bl*, 27*c*,
32*bl*, 34*tr/c*, 47*b*, 50*bl/tr*, 51*t*, 58-59;
Peter Dennis (Linda Rogers Associates) 4-5, 6-7*b*;
15, 20*b*, 21*tr*, 22*cl*, 23*t*, 34-37, 44*r*, 48*l/c*, 50-51*b*,
52-55, 56-57*c*; **Terry Gabbey** (Associated Freelance
Artists Ltd) 10-11, 18-19; **Jeremy Gower** 60-61;
Nicholas Hewetson 23*bl*; **Stephen Holmes** 41*tl*;
Adam Hook (Linden Artists) 42*b*, 44*cl*; 56*cl*;
Christa Hook (Linden Artists) 6-7*t*; 22, 25*tr*, 42*t*, 43*br*;
Tudor Humphries 39*r*; 45*tr*; 47*tr*;
John James (Temple Rogers Artists' Agents) 12-13,
26-31, 38; **Eddy Krähenbühl** 8-9, 16-17, 46*b*;
Nicki Palin 32-33*l/c*, 39*tl*, 40*r*, 41*r*;
Shirley Tourret (B.L. Kearley Ltd) 9*t*, 10*l*, 11*r*, 14*c/b*,
17*tr/br*, 20*tr*, 21*br*, 25*tl*, 27*bl*, 30, 33*bl/tr/c*; 34*bl*,
35*tr*, 36*t*, 37*br*, 39*tr*, 40*l*, 41*tr*, 43*tr*, 45*b*,
48*tr*, 49*tr*, 50*cl*, 54*l*, 56*l*, 57*r*
Woodcuts by **Anthony Colbert** (B.L. Kearley Ltd)
Border by **Kevin Kimber** (B.L. Kearley Ltd)

The publishers would also like to thank the following
for supplying photographs for this book:

Page 1 Bridgeman Art Library/Giraudon;
5 Mary Evans Picture Library;
6 Public Records Office;
13 Society of Antiquaries of London;
14 British Library *Royal MS 16 F11, folio 73*;
21 Bibliothèque Royale Albert
1er MS 9245 folio 254r;
27 Bridgeman Art Library/British Library
Add.19720 folio 214; 37 SCALA;
46 Bridgeman Art Library/Giraudon;
49 Bridgeman Art Library/Musée Condée;
53 British Library *Royal MS 14E IV folio 57*;
57 British Library *Royal MS 20C VII folio 41v*;
59 Royal Geographical Society